Approaching Pianowood Harbor

Books by Michael Spring

books

Blue Crow (LitPot Press, Inc., 2003)

Mudsong (Pygmy Forest Press, 2005)

Root of Lightning (Pygmy Forest Press, 2011)

Unfolding the Field (Left Fork, 2016)

dentro do som / inside the sound (Companhia das Ilhas, 2021)
Portuguese translation by Maria João Marques

Approaching Pianowood Harbor (Flowstone Press, 2025)

chapbooks

Dancing on Earth (M.A.F. Press, 1987)

Acoustic Trees (Arrowhead Press, 1988)

Light and Shadows

Moving Through Stone (Cyrano Press, 1999)

Gutter Therapy (Backer Editions, 1999)

Edge of Blue (Siski Press, 2002)

Blue Wolf (Dancing Moon Press, 2013)

Ravenwood (Left Fork, 2015)
with paintings by Deborah Ann Dawson

Drift Line (FootHills Publishing, 2020)

Kahlo's Window (SurVision Books, 2023)

children's book

Woodwoo - The Little Sasquatch (Left Fork, 2017)
illustrated by Deborah Ann Dawson

Copyright © 2025 Michael Spring
ISBN-13: 978-1-945824-68-5
Cover art by Jazmine Blu

First Left Fork Edition - April 2025

Approaching Pianowood Harbor

Michael Spring

July 26, 1963 — October 30, 2024

for my Jazzy

Eating Fish and Writing Poetry

Contents

foreword by John Amen   xiii

1

I leave behind the fool I've become	3
a gate fastened between two trees	4
chanterelle	5
sonata	6
rock wall	7
snowfield	8
fado	10
in the slow	11
my future selves won't give up	12
inside the drum	13
baladi	15
Madrone	16
drift line	18

2

recapturing poems	23
I see myself too old too soon	24
hopping the train	25
hospital walls, 3am	26
ocean inside the walls	27
you worry your clouds	28
now that the day stretches out like long sheep	29
lobster telephone	30
Pollock's dancer	31
mushroom casserole	32
the opposite of poverty	33
mango at dusk	34
Chevy Luv emerging	35
I went into the art museum	36
Azorean Saudade	37
Mambo Azul	38
into the mountain	39
in the low moan of the buoy's sound	40
after the king tide	41

3

Kahlo's window	47
how I see things	48
the magic ulu urges you	49
under the influence of Jung	50
after we climbed through the fence	51
the acrobat	52
into the tiger's mouth	53
the cry of her child rose	54
rope ladder made of bedsheets	55
tsunami	56
walking tree potion	57
rowing toward Pianowood Harbor	58
fish leapt from our eyes	59
glass mermaid	60
glass sculpture for the Wolf Moon	61
stone temple	62
turning pages	63
I open my hands to become birds	64
snake charmer	65
Jazmine and I with cobra lilies	66
because we read the poems of Rumi	67
under a new constellation	68
with her red skirt and sequins	69
dedications	70
acknowledgements	71
about the author	72
about Flowstone Press	74

foreword

Several years ago, during a phone conversation, Michael Spring told me that he was capturing rattlesnakes on his property in Oregon and relocating them to areas less inhabited by people. He stressed that, in his opinion, it was essentially the snakes' land that he and his family were now occupying. Relocating them with respect was the least he could do.

It's risky, of course, to mesh a poet's life and their work, to regard either one as too much of an influence on the other. That said, Spring's unsentimental yet reverent appreciation for nature, and its role in human development, was an integral part of his poetic work. There's an undeniable interdependence between humanity and earth, he suggests; we're made of the earth, the earth is made of us. We're inseparable. As early as 2005's *Mudsong*, Spring explored our relationship to the planet, vowing to be a steward of sorts:

> I walked past the Oregon ash
> and cattails
> through the soggy fields
> of tufted hairgrass
> ...
> I've decided
> I'm going to dedicate my life
> to this field
> and to its swamps and bogs
>
> ("mud song")

Later, in 2016's *Unfolding the Field*, he elaborated on this theme, finding balances between worldly involvement and moving past the clutter and debris of capitalistic fallout:

> The neighborhood dogs didn't hear me
> when I climbed over the fence
> and passed the yellow plastic Buddha
> and the smashed grocery cart tangled in ivy
>
> ... I followed the river
> over boulders and fallen trees
> into a field of tall grass
>
> ("walking away")

Here is a poet embracing a distinct minimalism to evoke a cathartic image of freedom. The poem, succinct as it is, captures an epic journey through a gauntlet of "neighborhood dogs", "brambles", "hobo camps", and "muck gripping tin cans". The concluding line offers a release; we can almost feel the clearing, the wind whipping freely. Spring's "field" is a contemporary revision of Rumi's field, of Romanticism's lauding of the natural order. It conjures Christianity's "new earth" and Buddhism's nibbana, the spaciousness and harmony we each seek in own way, barraged as we are by noise, obligations, and deadlines.

It's hard, as well, not to regard that field as a metaphor for death, the various images as illustrations of the hurdles we encounter on our way toward this inevitable (and yet, in Spring's depiction somewhat appealing or at least benevolent) destination. In his new/final works, we encounter Spring speaking more clearly and directly to the human malaise:

> fear is a basket
> inside our heads
> woven with colors so dazzling
> it's easy to get lost
>   ("ocean inside the walls")

He deftly avoided allusions to Greek mythology, zeroing in on the way in which the siren myth was always about our internal voices, not so much external temptation. What sweeps us into dangerous waters is not ultimately the world and its impositions but our own "fears", our own "heads" filled with pressing voices, concerns, and convincing "colors".

And yet, merging with the true self, the real world, God, life energy, however we might phrase it, and accessing the trust to surrender, became more and more important to Spring. In the exquisitely lyrical "under a new constellation", he offered,

> everything we own is moored
> to the dark water
> as the harbor a mile away
> cradles our sailboat
> everything we want
> sends sparks toward the stars
> together, we become
> a driftwood fire

And with the eccentrically sensual "stone temple", he concluded laconically yet complexly, "my jaguar simply wants / to run free with yours".

*

It's a profound experience when someone with whom we were close is suddenly and irreconcilably absent. I had the pleasure of working with Michael Spring for over fifteen years, editing various issues of *Pedestal Magazine*. He was a person who valued individuality, whether in life or artistic expression. He stood for justice, for people, the land, for the interconnectedness of species, for the value of aesthetics. He could be strikingly firm in a stance but also paradoxically flexible. Perhaps that was the result of his many years of immersion in the martial arts. He had an instinctive sense of how to proceed, what would best serve a given situation. I also think that long-term immersion in artistic processes (as an editor and poet) brings greater integrations. The opposites within us are somehow rendered complementary rather than incongruent. We become more fluid – in our art, hopefully in our lives as well.

I'll miss working with Michael, seeing where his poems would have gone next, hearing about his love for his wife, Jazmine. He was young, too young to go, and yet we often lose our loved ones before we're willing to let them depart (if we ever are). But Michael's was a life well-lived. He was true to the land and committed to artistic expression; he embraced successes, faced let-downs, experienced heartbreak and heart-fulfillment. I'm grateful that I had the opportunity to be his friend and colleague.

So we continue. We have our memories of Michael, we have his poems, and we'll march forward into our own fields, whatever they represent for us. Navigating our particular highs and lows, we'll stoke that "driftwood fire", the warmth and sense of belonging it provides. Moment by moment, we'll adhere to our higher callings.

—John Amen, January 2025

1

I leave behind the fool I've become

because I no longer talk to the azaleas
nor to the flowering dogwoods
nor to the thrushes or bees or earthworms

I'm afraid the world inside me
has no fish in the lakes, no visible stars
only smoldering cedars
and partial dreams sinking into partial dreams

I'm afraid I'll never again see the stone
buildings of my ancestral home
and I'll dissolve like a sand sculpture in the rain

that is why I've unplugged myself from my house
and I now lean over, listening
to this green moth on a green leaf

that is why I leave behind the fool I've become

I'm under the last street light
before the walkway over the river bridge
the green moth floats into open space
becomes the moon rising above the mountains

I can sense a new future self watching me
I know I will find him here on this path
where stone flows and folds away from the city
where rocks look like bones and internal organs
and the mossy trees look like breathing animals

a gate fastened between two trees

I scan the pines and ferns for cameras
for booby traps and no trespassing signs

there's no evidence of a fence
no evidence of anything else human

the gate's weave of branches are made
of snake-like pieces of madrone fastened with sinew

did someone whisper?
the shape of a tree becomes a person
a boulder the size of a bear seems to be breathing

if I were to walk through this gate
whose place might I be entering?
angel? demon? a madman wielding a chainsaw?

because I'm thinking this
I want to prove to myself there's nothing to fear

I create my own chasms:
a pit of snakes made from my flesh –
a burning river made of my blood

no, I won't be deterred
I unlatch the gate

chanterelle

> *Fr.: 'the singing one';*
> *The highest-pitched string of a stringed instrument*

because of the chanterelle we commune
with darkness – illuminating, transformative –
with our willow baskets we forage
between oaks and madrones through wet ferns

we move like mycelium
slowly, as muses whispering through fog

we hold our breath so we can hear their music –
perhaps it's synesthesia –
an association to their trumpet shapes –
but each one makes the sound of a violin

the chanterelles resemble flames made of flesh –
phototropic like hands in praise –

they push through leaf matter and moss –
their entire bodies are a nuptial of numinous forest webs –
they become songs we can consume

sonata

a field full of wooden statues –
women and men without faces –
each barely different from another –
their cupped hands filling with snow

I wait for what
will eventually touch the statues
and make them breathe

rock wall

my skull erodes
even as it forms

my heart is in the mouth
of another heart

I can hear thunder
from the river

the compacted snow
continuing to feed it

what draws me
to this wall?

my body
might be all I am

snowfield

now that the sky is the color of a blank page
and snow continues to fall

and because the darkness
of sleep is still with me

I open the door to winter

I step into a field of snow
and become a field of snow

last night snow
covered the details of yesterday, including
the unturned compost
and a stack of lumber for the unbuilt shed

snow changes things
as whitewash does
on a painted canvas –

even the garden beds
with their driftwood borders
are forming
into the shapes of slumbering bodies

slopes become shoulders and hips and thighs

I open my arms
and slowly turn in a circle
as if lost in a song
on a dancefloor

I'm one with snow's music –
more silence than sound – a quiet elation

similar to a child who discovers
another world in the feathery patterns
of frost on the window pane

I close my eyes
and observe myself observing myself

snow crystals form
and fall, latch and merge

become one landscape, one mind –

they float down
as the field before me stretches out –

widening in the drowse of milky clouds
as new pathways open through trees

fado

with lost love the Portuguese guitarist
soaks in a bathtub on a rooftop
pours himself another glass of vinho verde

then salutes twilight's last bawling gull
in a sky heavy with clouds

orange earth tones of rooftop tiles give way
to the darkening blues of cobbled streets

the guitarist can hear café chairs
scuffling, the alley below with laughter
and voices and ice clanking in glasses

garlic and salt rise into the belly of air
octopus sizzles on the grill

the guitarist knows it's time to climb out
of this bathwater and tune the strings

tonight Severa will sing fado: a moon
will emerge from the haze of the Tagus river
and because of fado

because it embraces fate and despair
the guitarist will sink into sound

he'll become the enchanted
fisherman, once again, casting
his interpretations of nets and hooks
into her songs

in the slow

she remembers how to speak
with her hands

with the underwater
sway of reeds

with clouds above
swimming with wind

because she stands waist deep
in the river's slow current

her hands stir the song
of the child she used to be

my future selves won't give up

even as I step outside the auditorium
into full sunlight

the Moonlight Sonata
lures me with its otherworldly light

even as I follow the glistening mud dauber wasp
to her clay pot construction

childhood memories of railroad tracks
and underground forts rise and materialize

I follow a rhythm of hammered strings
a cloud of shorebirds billow and surge

the music leads me into the forest
I will not stop walking

the bodies of my future selves
sway with the shadows of cedars and firs

inside the drum

a cache of pistachio shells and dog food nuggets
and confetti torn from the curled end of a grocery bag
and a fist-sized nest
of sofa insulation and carpet fibers

I don't want to believe it: mice have been inside my drum –
my sacred drum – a djembe carved
from African cherry wood

I left it lying on its side beside the bean bag chair

with paper towels
I wipe out the mouse droppings
I don't want to think about it:

instead of a rhythmic prayer from my hands, mice
have been making their tick tick sounds
with the tiny knives of their feet

I hit the drum hard, for exorcism
for its boom and thunder, for its pulse

I want the mice to pay for this invasion
I want to hear the traps snap like clap sticks
like flat stones slapping each other

but I know this is my fault – although I cherish
this drum, I've neglected it all summer

maybe I should be thankful instead –
the mice were simply following their own nature –

if not for them I wouldn't be
standing here, now,
running my fingers over the drumskin

I open my hands for the center of the drum
another big boom, but this time for my ancestors

for the Choctaw green corn dancers
for the twirling white dresses of the Portuguese festival
for the boy in the peat field stalking the Irish elk

I pat and slap and roll my fingers
the drum responds with white flames
with gold smoke

I close my eyes for flight – I'm singing without words –
I'm losing my mind, finally,
into this old way of dreaming

baladi

with this dumbek drum I play
for the belly dancer

for the silks and blades
of her body

a rhythm for her to swim
back to where she was born

she becomes a storm of birds
in a storm of leaves

the molting colors
under a gray whale sky

what sun is that inside the music?
what stirs the oceans now?

I drum I drum I dream
I enter the bleeding sunset

the dancer raises her arms
as if lifting a newborn child

Madrone

only a few days after her passing
I thought I saw her on the shore –

a young woman shielding her eyes
and squinting to see the explosive waves
against the sea stack

the beach seemed to breathe
waves flew apart in the wind

the sea stack
shimmered green on black

I picked up a folded knot of driftwood
that looked like a bird with an open beak –
there was a hole for an eye I could see through –
I held on to it

ahead of me was a galaxy
made of grainy sand and agates

below my feet an ant battled and freed itself
from a depression in the sand

because I was thinking of Madrone
as dawn's otherworldly purples and golds
darkened the sky, I believed there was a truth
being revealed – that she was everywhere

and suddenly everything I looked at
was amplified

I imagined the sea stack's birth
from Earth's mantle,
from magma eight centuries ago –
a plume of hissing steam and fire –
how it cracked silences into splinters

and now, to this day, the sea stack continues
to stand – a chthonic expression
towering above the surging breakers

it looks like a child in the distance –

it is Madrone as a child,
turned away from the shore, wading –
watching the shapeshifting clouds

drift line

we drag our heavy shadows as if we're sleepwalking
our heads bent as we shuffle across the sand

or we crawl on our hands and knees
or we sit and stare knowing we came here
to simply stretch out on the beach, not this!

the beach's giant sea stack looks
like a squatting frog with a periscopic eye
waves explode over its body as high tide approaches

we worry about the potential sneaker wave
but we don't lose focus on the drift line

we gather driftwood and petrified wood
chunks of metal   bones   shells
here's a sacrum and there's the disfigured pelvis
like wax forms warped from heat

there's a lion-faced woman
and a boot or the hilt of a sword
and this knotted piece makes the head of a crow
and this flare of wood makes a pair of wings

we're here with a dozen other beachcombers
transfixed, illuminated, akin to Tibetan monks
with their woven bags full of colored sand

the hovering shorebirds might see us as part
of a multihued mandala
as we shuffle and crawl, undeterred

and nothing would deter us – nothing!
even if a whale surged onto the beach and opened
its cavernous mouth
as long as there was a continued line
of treasures, we would enter

and perhaps we have –
perhaps we're in such a darkness now, believing
we're still collecting what the ocean brought us

I feel a shifting beneath our feet
as if the whale slides back into the surf

there's the crash of waves
there it is again   and again

2

recapturing poems

some of the poems that break
out of my head hit the ground

then crawl to the edge of a garden
or slither under scrap metal in a garage

like legless iguanas or featherless birds
or spiders with too many legs

and some of them take to the wind
like papery skinned fish or ballooning frogs
and I lose them forever

but this is my process as I get the chance
to see what a few of them actually look like

for those that survive and I'm able to recapture
I place in one of the drawers in my chest
or spine or between my legs or armpits

I place them in whatever drawers
contain trapped traumas or emotions

sometimes the poems form into the creatures
they were born to be

but only if I can find that particular place
in my body that will nourish them

I see myself too old too soon

in this room of must and old books
and ashy smoke from the fireplace
I'll probably age on this rickety
folding chair and lose my ability to read
even these words I'm writing now

I'll squint over the table making up dice games
to divert me from the feeling
of mediocrity of course I'd rather be
elevating my life with chess, but I lose
most games now, even when I play myself

I'm like a cello trying to play itself

hey, wait a minute – there's hope after all –
I didn't expect I'd see myself
as a cello

hopping the train

between Porky's Café
and Gravy's Autowreckers
the train switches tracks toward Vegas

coyote in the distance watches me
pace the tracks
I scuffle dust as I measure my run

I'm not sure what I'd do if I get caught
they toss people from trains
to discourage train hopping

it's a crap shot whether someone lives or dies
the closest thing I have to a gun
is a rusted railroad spike

I'll take my chances gambling
maybe I'll land a circus job

I want to be a wildcard
like this coyote
who leaps into thickets
becomes tumbleweed
becomes a dust devil
becomes everything I'm after

hospital walls, 3am

after the pulmonary embolism

the walls are made of wings rustling inside the white paint
my wife is asleep in a foldout chair in the corner of the room

my body is sunk into pillows facing a dark TV screen –
a black mirror – I watch myself and her

and all the pulsing monitors floating behind us –
their lights turn the walls into folds of ocean slabs

what I thought were wings a few minutes ago
might be fins and coral and wrack

I see myself swimming in all of this –
I'm calibrating myself to this new way of breathing –

I sink and surface
sink
and surface …

ocean inside the walls

now inside our floorboards, the ocean
is lapping our bedframe
too close to our dreams

we want the ocean
but we fear being submerged too long

we worry our dreams are at risk
of drowning

fear is a basket
inside our heads
woven with colors so dazzling
it's easy to get lost

as if we were on a boat without navigation devices
and without stars

all the boats inside us
want too much
to open their sails and flee

the crash of sky and thunder of surf
is what stirs them

we need to convince them
we contain the ocean they need

we need to keep what boats we still have
at bay

you worry your clouds

you worry your clouds
in your paintings look too much
like clouds rather than portals

but when I look into your paint
I get lost, my imagination stirs –
I enter the tangles of a rain forest
and feel the blue heat
of a sleeping volcano

crimson and gold pour over my skin –
colors slash and dance
as if borne from a magician's wand

everything appears mercurial –
a metal building tears apart
into flapping birds
a tree bends into an octopus, slides
into the ocean

because you worry your clouds
everything in their shadows appear
to coagulate, transmute

I now see that a mushroom
is more like a mother king cobra
after forming a nest for her eggs

or more like a monk sipping milk
from the moon
than a monkey eating fruit

now that the day stretches out like long sheep

I unfold the book of surrealism
into a picnic table

words from the book
have rolled into tiny globsters
and now wriggle like fat grubs

a multitude of hungry crows breaks
out of my head
to feast

lobster telephone

because you've turned the phone into a lobster I have a hard time
handling its carapace, slippery as its telson thrashes and slaps air

I can hear your voice, but I can't press my ear close to the crustacean
and to all those scrabbling legs and swimmerets

the lobster's large claws work on lopping off my ear
its mandibles maw and its maxillipeds and antennules wriggle
    as I ask you
Can you turn the phone into something else? Maybe call me back
    on another line?
I look at its gawping eyes as its antennae whip back and forth
what else can I do but do what's best for the lobster
I take it to the water's edge and let go

Pollock's dancer

at least six dancers simultaneously caught
but there is only one
oscillating on each side of the moment

the dancer's body sways in a field
of fibrous reeds
as threads of sunlight fly

from her clavicle
from her elbows and knees
and from her bent and outstretched fingers

as a dumbek drummer pulled from shadow
I no longer want to make sense
my hands drum lightning from skin

inside this polymorphic dance
my song unravels, pulsates, splatters light
in every direction

awakening the tongues inside the reeds

mushroom casserole

no, I didn't see the bear today
near the ancient apple tree

nor did I unfold my beach chair
to fish the pond

I couldn't stop writing in my journal
I didn't leave the house

I'm sorry I haven't yet returned
your call

the sun has set, the moon is bright
and I'm still in my pajamas

I haven't harvested the boletes
fruiting near the woodpile

although they are inside
my head, sizzling in a skillet, so delicious

the opposite of poverty

is slow rumba in stereo
as a couple in their apartment
practice dance steps
in striped underwear

they move with the percussion
of a conga seducing a guitar

above the couch is a painting
of a woman holding a candle
descending the stairs for a man
made of smoke

smoke from a rose-red candle
moves out the window
into a blue night

from dark trees
the moon releases an owl

mango at dusk

I believed, briefly I was made
of the ocean's
red and orange hues at dusk

sticky mango sluiced
my face and hands
as sweet juice found my tongue

the ocean appeared fleshy
I wanted to spend my life
with its textures and stirring currents

I tore into the mango – it was a poem
I devoured (always looking for that poem!)
finding more of this world to love

Chevy Luv emerging

the engine hangs from a hook
outside its body

my friend examines it
and everything else left
under the hood – still full
of disconnected hoses and wires

clamps and washers
are scattered at his feet
metal tools shimmer in a black case

for this kind of surgery
he doesn't wear gloves

greasy work –
oil instead of blood

this truck would've sunk
into the scrapyard, disappear
but he has the battery
charging on a pedestal

he will pound out the dents, sand
and repaint it

my friend sees this truck
as much of a living thing –
important work – his life
somehow absorbed into the metal

I went into the art museum

I went into the art museum to find
the painting you said was you
I went inside its mushroom-shaped cromlech
to see us together as children again
to see us as if we were in our underground fort
I went in to see us lighting the candles
I went in to see us melting our plastic soldiers
we wanted to misshapen them
we wanted to make them monsters and superheroes
we were tired of the televised war
we had other wars to think about
we had no idea you'd lose your life in a war
when you disappeared from the cromlech
I ran outside to follow
I looked for you hiding in the grass
I looked for you in the sky
I finally saw you burning in the sunset
I watched you melt
I watched you dribble down the grassy hill
I watched you form into a door
and when I opened the door
I found myself outside the painting
the painting was floating on the white wall
I found myself touching the wooden frame
I imagined I was touching your face
the cromlech was no longer a cromlech
it was a mushroom made of glass panels
it was a mushroom with a thousand eyes
there was a boy inside the mushroom
there was a boy inside with flames for fingers

Azorean Saudade

while looking across the scramble of lava rock
and beyond it the sea stack in explosive surf
you hold a blue hydrangea
and lift it toward no one I can see

waves explode against the sea stack
I call out to you
you lift the flower toward no one I can see
Vamberto, she is no longer here

I call out to you
as I walk across the dock's creaking planks
Vamberto, she is no longer here
among the gurgling engines of fishing boats

I approach you on the creaking planks
you tell me I am wrong
among the gurgling engines of fishing boats
she is here, she will always be on this island

Yes, Vamberto, I am wrong
we are looking across the scramble of lava rock
she is here, she will always be on this island
where you stand, holding a blue hydrangea

Mambo Azul 3am

after a painting by Elizabeth Buchter

she waded through cattails
and stood waist deep in the pond

her skin absorbed the blue of dusk

when she opened her hand
to release a ghost

swamp trees encroached
with hunger

a black moon burned
inside her

from death and decay
to light
she sang

that is when the shadows
dissolved in the water
and the water began to stir

then as she pulled the pond
like a robe over her shoulders

lily pads and koi
drifted
the contours of her body

into the mountain

the way the velvet ant pulls
my attention to follow her
scarlet light under a flap of moss

the way an amethyst
cracked from a thunder egg
takes my mind
into visceral crystalline landscapes

I enter the mountain
into the past
no, it is the present   or future

into the ancient light   of darkness
where sound and scent build landscapes
and mountain pathways

where I can finally see myself
as animal   as particles   as numerous
elements   as the world

in the low moan of the buoy's sound

like anything can be
it is a door –

downed – I sleep sound –
in the blanket I find inside

after the king tide

we have come here to find something symbolic
to inform our relationship

we look at clumps of seaweed like we would tea leaves
and into driftwood like I Ching sticks
and at agates as black mirrors

so high on the beach we never knew
the water could reach
we find a stingray torn open
by some sharp-toothed thing
and parts of an octopus
colorless and languid against rocks

could we end up as this octopus?
or one of the indecipherable lumped shapes
buried in the sand?

we see crushed and dismantled crab pots

and a sea bass who died eating another sea bass –
one head inside the other –
their tails like fans on each side
of their bloated bodies

but where is that symbolic thing?

perhaps it is that golf ball over there – gold
like this morning's sunrise –

and there's another … and another –
yes, this must be it!

because we can see so many scattered about the beach
we begin to hunt for every last one

3

Kahlo's window

although I didn't choose
to become this stony ground
I might as well try
to change

as the vast landscape of volcanic rock
begins to eat another village
a window opens in the middle
of my chest

a tangle of grapevines
pours out

blood through leaf veins
seeps into the ground

how I see things

my eye is a mouth holding an egg
if I stand still long enough I'll have the guts
to swallow my future

the magic ulu urges you

you lop off the head
of a barracuda
for the stars
held in its eyes

you don't know
if you can grow stars
but you have this soil
and you have these eyes

under the influence of Jung

tonight the black sky is an ocean
I sit at the bottom looking up
as moonlit clouds become dive boats

what if divers from that surface
dove down to see what I am? I'd slip away
into the things I love in this world

I'd be a single thread of music in a symphony
a wing of moss on a mountain of moss
a rock in a field of rocks

inside the rock there is a secret passageway
(as everything has) as the path evolves
into a dragon in a river of stars

after we climbed through the fence

freight cars blasted by with a rush of wind
and screaming metal

box cars, hopper cars, empty livestock cars
graffiti slipping past us

what we really wanted to see
was a livestock car with an elephant or a giraffe
or a flatcar full of slumbering contortionists

we hoped to see someone thrown from the train
who'd tell us the octopus woman
thought he was the best acrobat she ever saw

and perhaps he'd also say life
in the circus was worth it

the acrobat

after the show she enters
the walk-in closet in her bedroom
turns the lights off and shuts the door

no iron rings or blades to juggle
no ropes to balance upon, no bears
to dance with, no zebras to mount

no dazzling lights and faces, no human eyes
upon her as if she were a sandwich
for all that hunger

in this room there's nothing
to jump though, fly from or into
there's only a mattress on the floor

and the total darkness
her body will finally absorb

into the tiger's mouth

of course I'll continue
sticking my head into the tiger's mouth

as long as the crowd continues
to cram forward with their tickets

as long as fear presses them together
as one lump of clay

where I can knead then shape them
into an enormous set of hands

one to hold the tiger's mouth open
and the other to pull me free

the cry of her child rose

by the time Pope Joan revealed
she was a she

she had already broken
open –

a thousand pigeons
feathered the sky –

it was too late for the stunned
cardinals to hide her

her sky blue robe collapsed
during the public procession

a placenta and amniotic fluid
pooled on the garden path

St. Peters Cathedral opened
her eyes

Pope John is Pope Joan
Pope Joan is a mother

the sun flipped like a tossed coin
electricity sizzled in the clouds

rope ladder made of bedsheets

to escape the mundane
I climb out the apartment window
three stories high to the street below

when my feet meet the ground
it's like entering a door randomly placed
on a park bridge to a flamingo pond
or a miniature golf course

if you saw such a door standing alone
on a path or in the middle of a field
wouldn't you walk through? imagine

how different your world might be –
imagine your miniature golf ball
expanding to the size of a human head
exploding off the tee – a perfect stroke –

gagging the throat
of the goblin who wants to eat you

tsunami

the boats broken from their moorings
look like drunk horses trying to find
their way around the docks

but the docks come undone too
as the water rose so subtly
no one seemed alarmed

several miles of rising
water still coming
as boats bang against other boats

and floating cars in the parking lot
and here they come – a pride of sea lions
flipping around in the water

they are thrashing the surface
bumbling over boats, tipping
them over – catching a ride

on the floodwaters
toward the sinking fresh fish market –
they are dunking cars along the way

barking, howling as they bounce –
blubber over metal –
they've waited a long time for this

walking tree potion

I poured a gallon of lagoon water
into the banyan tree barrel

and began humming a frequency
only the earthworms know

when I drink this potion
I will be committing myself
to the ligneous

I will be ready for the ground
to stir

if you stay you will see me
wallowing in the compost

my mind will branch
adnate to the moist and viscid threads
of the forest

you will see my body finally stretch
into the shape of a tree

I will begin walking
making my way back
into the world

rowing toward Pianowood Harbor

the harbor master boasts most of it
was built from planks meant for pianos

including the hotel and diner

how many pianos might have existed
from the wood that built this harbor?

the one in the piano bar reverberates
the melodic voices in the room

when I land I might find luck
in this place – I am rowing –

I have heard the cautions
about the acoustics in the dining room –

I am rowing there now

to your table where I will risk falling
in love with every word you speak

fish leapt from our eyes

they flashed into gray water
frothing it into a fiery
cyanescent frenzy of dancing forms

merfolk playfully frolicked
with each other
flipping in and out of the sea

we both claimed we wanted
to take things slower

but, oh, those damned fish –
of course we dove in!

glass mermaid

so that her glass body doesn't crack
she anneals in the oven
as her torso fuses with her dichroic tail

if her body were a wine glass
it would sing with a wet fingertip

most nights tending the oven I sip red wine
with a violin quartet on the radio
or with a woman singing fado

but tonight I pour a glass of vinho verde
and wait in silence as the mermaid is resting

the dichroic shimmers
a thousand metallic colors
like the sun brings out on fish scales

the mermaid has yet to sing
I would risk drowning to hear her

glass sculpture for the Wolf Moon

she hands me the wolf
she sculpted with fire and glass

transparent with cobalt blue
glass like smoke inside the wolf's core

as I hold it to light the blue ignites
a cumulous cloud

a churning mass of weather
it is a moon in utero

it is what forms in the moment before
the wolf lifts its head to howl

as I lift the sculpture to my eyes
I see reflections

I see the bottle of red wine before us
and the books wavery against the walls

I see the pinks and browns of her skin
swimming inside the wolf's blues

the walls vanish, and the bottle of wine
floats into her hand

my dream body enters her dream body
her dream body enters mine

stone temple

it seems impossible your jaguar slipped in unnoticed
before the stone doors were sealed

I will pry the door open for you
but you must promise your jaguar won't attack mine

my jaguar simply wants
to run free with yours

turning pages

because she tells me the sound
of turning pages arouses her
I can't recall what page I originally wanted
to show her

all that matters now is this sound – this susurrus –
this soft plosive sigh as a page lifts
and falls –

a sheet of paper peels back for another –
my fingers slide across the paper
as if it were her skin

I open my hands to become birds

fear makes me doubt
your hands will not be birds, but you
have already shown them to me

I shouldn't doubt
what I see –

an entire forest of birds!

snake charmer

every time I say her name
aloud
    a snake pours out
    of my mouth –

and because of my
profession
    I am one
    of the luckiest men alive

Jazmine and I with cobra lilies

we are on our hands and knees in a bog of cobra lilies
to another observer we might appear to be lapping seep
from the cobra-like heads

as the plants begin to twitch and sway
winged insects buzz, bang against its inner walls
we are strange cat-like apes crawling the seeping slope

when we finally wrap around each other
we will become the entire buzzing bog of cobra lilies
we, too, will begin to twitch and sway

because we read the poems of Rumi

on a blanket near the river
we entered
an imaginary cave
where we built

a driftwood fire
and as the fire grew
the walls around us
began to breathe

under a new constellation

everything we own is moored
to the dark water

as the harbor a mile away
cradles our sailboat

everything we want
sends sparks toward the stars

together, we become
a driftwood fire

with her red skirt and sequins

she flames on the wick of the Celtic bodhran's rhythm
as the hurdie gurdie with flutes and guitars build
a ladder I now climb
leading into the wing bones
of the house – yes, our
house can fly!

dedications

"Mambo Azul" is for Elizabeth Buchter

"after we climbed through the fence"
is for my cousin Kevin Garcia

"Chevy Luv emerging" is for Eddie Burdette

"Madrone" is for Bill Jackson

"the opposite of poverty" is for John Harn

"Azorean Saudade" is for Vamberto Freitas

"snowfield," "rock wall," and "chanterelle"
are for Joe Armstrong and the people of the Shire

"under the influence of Jung" is for my dad Dean Spring

"drift line" and "in the slow" are for Kate Taormina

And several poems, often obvious,
are for my wife Jazmine Blu

acknowledgements

With many thanks to the editors of the following publications where several poems in this book first appeared, sometimes in different versions:

Alchemy Spoon (UK): the cry of her child rose
Blue Mountain Review: Madrone
Crannog (Ireland): fado
Eunoia Review (Singapore): after we climbed through the fence; how I see things; Jazmine and I with cobra lilies; mushroom casserole; stone temple; with her red skirt and sequins
Feral: A Journal of Poetry and Art: lobster telephone
Gargoyle: snowfield; inside the drum
Gavea-Brown: Azorean Saudade; glass mermaid
Hamilton Stone Review: drift line: I leave behind the fool I have become
Inflectionist Review: in the slow; sonata; rock wall
Neologism: into the tiger's mouth
New York Quarterly: hopping the train
Otoliths (Australia): a gate fastened between two trees; into the mountain
Paris/Atlantic (France): the magic ulu urges you
South Florida Poetry Journal: the opposite of poverty
SurVision (Ireland): because we read the poems of Rumi; I open my hands to become birds; I went into the art museum; Kahlo's window; snake charmer; under a new constellation; walking tree potion;
The Journal of Compressed Creative Arts: the acrobat
Turtle Island Quarterly: baladi; Chevy Luv emerging; glass sculpture for the Wolf Moon; Mambo Azul; mango at dusk; rowing toward Pianowood Harbor; tsunami; under the influence of Jung

Some of the poems have been reprinted in the following publications: *Azoriano Oriental Arts & Letras* (Portugal), *Cobra Lily, Into the Azorean Sea*; *Bilingual Anthology of Azorean Poetry, Three Rivers Chorale, Takilma Common Ground, Insider of Southern Oregon*, and *Vita Brevis*.

Thanks to everyone who helped with the poems in this book, particularly for my mentor Sara Backer, and to Jazmine Blu and Barbara Parchim. Thanks to Marcy and Katherine Tilton for their retreat at Chez Tilton. Thanks to DISQUIET International for the Azorean residency. Thanks to Joe Armstrong and his Shire where this book began. Thanks to Sarah Meyer and her Harbor House where this book was completed.

about the author

Michael Spring was the author of numerous poetry books and chapbooks and one children's book. His most recent poetry book was *dentro do som / inside the sound* (Companhia das Ilhas, Portugal, 2021). His latest chapbook *Kahlo's Window* (SurVision Books, 2023) won the James Tate Prize. Other poetry awards he received include The Robert Graves Award, The Turtle Island Poetry Award, runner-up for the Paris Book Festival Award, and an honorable mention for the Eric Hoffer Book Award. He was also a recipient of a Luso-American Fellowship from DISQUIET International. His poems appeared in numerous publications, including: *Atlanta Review*, *Crannog*, *Flyway*, *Gavea-Brown*, *The Midwest Quarterly*, *NEON*, *New York Quarterly*, *Paris/Atlantic*, Poetry New Zealand, and *Spillway*. He was a poetry editor for *The Pedestal Magazine* and founding Editor-in-Chief of Flowstone Press. *Approaching Pianowood Harbor*, Michael's final book of poetry, earned Honorable Mention in the 2024 Sally Albiso Poetry Book Awards.

Flowstone Press was founded by Michael Spring and Ryan Forsythe in 2016 with a goal of publishing contemporary poetry collections and chapbooks, focusing on lyrical, psychological, environmental, cultural, and imagistic work. Mike selected the poetry and worked with each author while Ryan completed the layout and design work. Before he passed in October 2024, Michael was working on the 30th Flowstone book, *Voices of the Valley*, with co-edtior Steven Sher. Steven and Ryan have worked to complete this last project in Michael's honor. He had also completed his last poetry manuscript, *Approaching Pianowood Harbor*. These two will be the final books from the press. Below we present the complete listing of books published by Michael's Flowstone Press.

2016
River of Solace - Gary Lark
Desultory Sonnets - Ted Jean
The Wire Fence Holding Back the World - Martin Willitts, Jr.

2017
Bright Darkness - Ken Letko
Announcements from the Planetarium - Judith Arcana
Laying By - Vincent Wixon
Life's Prisoners - Darryl Lorenzo Wellington
Ghost Logic - Sara Clancy
Shadows Within the Roaring Fork - Jared Smith

2018
Stem of Us - Carter McKenzie
Obsession with the Dogwood - Jane Blue
Growing Smaller - Coreen Davis Hampson
Message from the Vessel in a Dream - Christopher Luna

2019
Such Luck - Sara Backer

2020
show me something you can not even think of - Elena Botts
Moving with Every - Dan Raphael
Daybreak on the Water - Gary Lark

2021
Chopping Wood in the Moonlight - Ken Letko
Anatomy of a Wound - Lorrie Ness
What Remains - Barbara Parchim
Psalms at the Present Time - Darryl Lorenzo Wellington

2022
Watering the Rhubarb - Charles Goodrich
Mostly the Wind - John Harn
What if Your Mother (2nd Edition) - Judith Arcana
Pulse and Weave - Liz Nakazawa
Not Only the Extraordinary are Entering the Dream World - Martin Willitts, Jr.

2023
Three Chapbooks, Three Poets - Rodger Moody, Carol Durak, John P Harn

2024
Heritage & Other Pseudonyms - Lorrie Ness
Muscle Tree - Barbara Parchim

2025
Voices of the Valley: The Corvallis Poetry Anthology -
Michael Spring & Steven Sher, eds.

Approaching Pianowood Harbor - Michael Spring

www.ingramcontent.com/pod-product-compliance
Lightning Source LLC
Chambersburg PA
CBHW061810070526
44586CB00024B/2789